ENCOUNTERS WITH JESUS

Encounters with Jesus

David E. Rosage

SERVANT BOOKS
Ann Arbor, Michigan

Published by Servant Books
P.O. Box 8617
Ann Arbor, Michigan 48107

Cover design by Gerald Gawronski

Printed in the United States of America
ISBN 0-89283-368-8

87 88 89 90 91 92 10 9 8 7 6 5 4 3 2 1

In Gratitude

To
the angelic messengers
prophets
seers
wise men
priests
parents
teachers
and everyone who led me to the Word of God
and above all to
Jesus, the Word of the Father.

Contents

Introduction

Why does the transcendent God of heaven and earth, the Creator and Sustainer of the entire universe, the God of Abraham, Isaac, and Jacob, want to communicate with us personally and individually?

In addition to the inspirations and insights given us daily by the Holy Spirit, our loving Father uses the medium of his written Word as found in the Scriptures to speak to us. His Word has been spoken to us down through the ages by angelic messengers, prophets, and seers. The tremendous climax of his revealed Word is personified in his Son, Jesus.

God's Word is actually a revelation of himself and his divine attributes, illuminated by his unconditional love for each one of us. In the Scriptures we discover countless golden nuggets of inspiration to guide us, to motivate and encourage us, to comfort and reassure us on our journey through life.

In addition to increasing our faith, enkindling our hope, and inflaming our love, God's Word acquaints us with some special people whom the Lord has called to accomplish his purpose by fulfilling a particular role in his plan of salvation. Their response to the Lord's invitation and their firm commitment and dedication challenge us to do likewise.

In *Encounters with Jesus* we will meet a number of these people who fulfilled a specific role in the preparation and coming of Jesus into the world. We rejoice with all of them, from Zechariah and Elizabeth to Simeon and Anna. When we get better acquainted with them, we find that they had the same fears and doubts which we experience. They had to overcome hardships similar to those which beset us. They had to step out in faith, not knowing where the Lord was leading them nor what the future held in store.

This volume is a collection of meditations addressed to some of the people who played a vital role in the events surrounding the Nativity. Directing a meditation to each one individually is a very personal method of becoming acquainted and communicating with them. It will bring us into a deeper appreciation of their fidelity to the mission to which they were called. It will also make us more aware of the fruits we are enjoying because of their dedication. As we get to know their minds and hearts, we will find inspiration and support in our own struggles.

As we identify with these privileged people, they will become our spiritual companions, enriching our lives. As we share our thoughts and feelings with them, they will surely assist us by their powerful intercession from their place on high.

Try thinking of each of these meditations as a personal letter, written by you to the biblical personage addressed in the Scripture. With only a casual or rapid perusal of these "letters," you may think that some have a more formal closing while others may seem to end rather abruptly. This was done for a purpose. Hopefully the thoughts expressed in them will lead us into some kind of reflective prayer, and on into the contemplative prayer posture of listening with the heart.

If we are drawn into the prayer of listening, we simply rest in awe and amazement at the fidelity of God in keeping his promise to send us a "Savior, the Messiah and Lord." In quiet wonder we behold the mysterious unfolding of God's divine designs in the preparation and the coming of his only-begotten Son in the Incarnation.

In silence and solitude we may wish to permit the boundless love of the Lord to penetrate more deeply into our hearts. When that takes place, our response will naturally be a paean of great praise and joyous thanksgiving.

Thinking of these meditations as letters may strike us as an unusual approach to the Bible, but it will make the message of the Lord to us more personal. Occasionally in our prayer time, we may wish to write a note or letter to some biblical personage. It will enrich our own relationship with them and also with the Lord. We may even receive a response in some fashion.

Gospel of Joy

Many have undertaken to compile a narrative of the events which have been fulfilled in our midst, precisely as those events were transmitted to us by the original eyewitnesses and ministers of the word.

I too have carefully traced the whole sequence of events from the beginning, and have decided to set it in writing for you, Theophilus, so that Your Excellency may see how reliable the instruction was that you received. (Lk 1:1-4)

ONE

Portrait of Jesus

"Many have undertaken to compile a narrative of the events which have been fulfilled in our midst, precisely as those events were transmitted to us by the original eyewitnesses and ministers of the word." (Lk 1:1-2)

Luke, your Gospel points out many wonderful features of the way of life which Jesus taught and lived himself. Your writings radiate great joy. Christianity is a religion of joy.

The births of John the Baptist and Jesus are announced with great joy and elicit joy in the hearts of all people. Whenever you record an act of repentance and forgiveness, you are certain to mention the joy which followed. Jesus says: "I tell you, there will likewise be more joy in heaven over one repentant sinner than over ninety-nine righteous people who have no need to repent" (Lk 15:7). The return of the prodigal son was hailed with an elaborate celebration. You end your Gospel with the disciples' returning to Jerusalem "filled with joy" after the ascension (Lk 24:52).

There is another cause for joy which permeates your whole Gospel. You tell us in no uncertain terms that God wants the salvation of all people. You give the Samaritans the assurance that the kingdom of heaven is open to them also, even though the orthodox Jews considered them heretical. You relate the parable of the Good Samaritan (Lk 10:30-37). Of the ten lepers whom Jesus cured, only one returned to thank him and "This man was a Samaritan" (Lk 17:11-19).

You were also solicitous about the Gentiles. Your words bring much consolation to them since you insist that they too are included in the universal salvation Jesus came to bring. The orthodox Jews of your time believed that no Gentile could ever be saved. Yet you portray Jesus as speaking with approval of the Gentiles: the widow of Zarephath and Naaman, the Syrian (Lk 4:25-27). Jesus also praised the faith of the Roman centurion (Lk 7:1-10).

Radiating from your verbal portrait of Jesus is his loving mercy, compassion, and forgiveness. Your account of Jesus gives us much hope and trust in him. The parable of the prodigal son (Lk 15:11) and the story of Jesus dealing with the penitent woman in the home of Simon (Lk 7:36) are only two of the many encounters Jesus had with sinners. In your Gospel, his compassionate forgiveness of them comes to life.

You also portrayed Jesus as a healer. In fact, you record more of Jesus' healings than any other evangelist. As soon as Jesus began his public ministry, he reached out in loving concern for the poor, the downtrodden, the sick, lepers, and cripples of every sort. Jesus always healed the whole person. He healed physically, spiritually, and mentally.

I need to remember that this type of ministry was not considered honorable at that time because the people believed that all sickness and misfortune were punishments from God. Any sufferer was regarded as a sinner and had to be avoided. Jesus broke down that false barrier. Thanks to you, Luke, we can see another facet of the heart of Jesus.

You also made Jesus known as a person of infinite patience, telling us of his receiving and blessing little children when he was exhausted after a full day's ministry (Lk 18:16). On the road to Emmaus, he manifested his patience with his disciples who were so slow to understand (Lk 24:13). How patiently and laboriously Jesus dealt with the enemies who dogged his footsteps, eager to trap him in his teachings.

TWO

Teach Us to Pray

"So that Your Excellency may see how reliable the instruction was that you received." (Lk 1:4)

Luke, your Gospel has been rightly called the Gospel of prayer. In the Nativity narratives, you record four magnificent prayers. After the birth of John the Baptizer, his father, Zechariah, uttered his memorable prophetic canticle. During the visit of Mary to Elizabeth, Mary poured forth her heart in a hymn of praise and joy which is used daily in the church today. We can hear the voices of the heavenly host singing the praises of God as they announced the Good News to the shepherds. The prayer of Simeon's joyful submission to the Lord impresses us deeply. Praise is a high form of prayer, and your Gospel leads us into the prayer of praise.

At all the great moments in the life of Jesus, you

show Jesus at prayer, in order to show us the value and necessity of prayer in our lives. Jesus prayed liturgically as he joined his own people in the synagogue. Jesus went to "the synagogue on the sabbath as he was in the habit of doing" (Lk 4:16).

Jesus also prayed privately and contemplatively. "He went out to the mountain to pray, spending the night in communion with God" (Lk 6:12).

On at least three occasions, Jesus asked his prayer team to pray with him. One such occasion occurred when Jesus was trying to ascertain if this was the time that he should go up to Jerusalem to begin his mission of suffering. "He [Jesus] took Peter, John and James, and went up onto a mountain to pray" (Lk 9:28).

You also tell us that Jesus paused many times to lift his mind and heart to his Father in heaven. At the Last Supper, Jesus "offered a blessing in thanks" (Lk 22:17). Jesus found comfort and consolation in prayer during his dreadful agony in the garden of Gethsemane. "In his anguish he prayed with all the greater intensity" (Lk 22:44). When the disciples asked: "Lord, teach us to pray," he taught them and us the Lord's Prayer (Lk 11:1ff).

I appreciate also your mention of Mary praying fervently with the early church for the outpouring of the Holy Spirit. Luke, you are careful to point out that in the Upper Room before the descent of the Holy Spirit, "There were some women in their company, and Mary the Mother of Jesus" (Acts 1:14). We can well imagine how ardently Mary prayed for the release of the Holy Spirit upon the first members of the church. She continues to do so today.

Announcement of the
Birth of John

In the days of Herod, king of Judea, there was a priest named Zechariah of the priestly class of Abijah; his wife was a descendant of Aaron named Elizabeth. Both were just in the eyes of God, blamelessly following all the commandments and ordinances of the Lord. They were childless, for Elizabeth was sterile; moreover, both were advanced in years.

Once, when it was the turn of Zechariah's class and he was fulfilling his functions as a priest before God, it fell to him by lot according to priestly usage to enter the sanctuary of the Lord and offer incense. While the full assembly of people was praying outside at the incense hour, an angel of the Lord appeared to him, standing at the right of the altar of incense. Zechariah was deeply disturbed upon seeing him, and overcome by fear.

The angel said to him: "Do not be frightened, Zechariah; your prayer has been heard. Your wife Elizabeth shall bear a son whom you shall name John. Joy and gladness will be yours, and many will rejoice at his birth; for he will be great in the eyes of the Lord. He will never drink wine or strong drink, and he will be filled with the Holy Spirit from his mother's womb. Many of the sons of Israel will he bring back to the Lord their God. God himself will go before him, in the spirit and power of Elijah, to turn the hearts of fathers to their children and the rebellious to the wisdom of the just, and to prepare for the Lord a people well-disposed."

Zechariah said to the angel: "How am I to know this? I am an old man; my wife too is advanced in age." The angel replied; "I am Gabriel, who stand in attendance before God. I was sent to speak to you and bring you this good news. But now you will be mute—unable to speak—until the day these things take place, because you have not trusted my words. They will all come true in due season." Meanwhile, the people were waiting for Zechariah, wondering at his delay in the temple. When he finally came out he was unable to speak to them, and they realized that he had seen a vision inside. He kept making signs to them, for he remained speechless.

Then, when his time of priestly service was over, he went home. Afterward, his wife Elizabeth conceived. She went into seclusion for five months, saying: "In these days the Lord is acting on my behalf: he has seen fit to remove my reproach among men." (Lk 1:5-25)

THREE

Vision at the Incense Hour

"Your wife Elizabeth shall bear a son whom you shall name John." (Lk 1:13)

You must have been thrilled, Zechariah, to be chosen by lot to enter the sanctuary of the Lord to offer incense along with the prayers of all the people. This was a great privilege, not given to every priest because of the great numbers of priests serving the Lord.

Only those men who were direct descendants of Aaron could be priests, so you had every reason to be proud of your lineage and vocation in life. But this was not your only blessing. In order to safeguard the lineage, a priest had to marry a woman of pure Jewish blood. It was even more praiseworthy to marry a woman like Elizabeth who was also a direct descendant of Aaron.

However, tragedy stalked you throughout your married life. You had no son to succeed you in the priesthood.

This was a terrible tragedy, for the customs and culture of your times maintained that childlessness was a manifestation of God's disfavor. In fact, a Jew who had no children could be considered excommunicated from God. Childlessness was valid grounds for divorce. I am sure you were thinking about this, as you prepared to enter into the sanctuary of the Lord to offer incense on this day. Elizabeth's childlessness had been uppermost in your prayer for many long years.

When you offered incense and saw the angel, you were deeply disturbed and overcome with fear. It was an overwhelming experience to behold an angel of the Lord. Your vision was awe-inspiring, but you were even more thrilled at the message of the angel. "Your wife Elizabeth shall bear a son whom you shall name John. Joy and gladness will be yours, and many will rejoice at his birth; for he will be great in the eyes of the Lord. . . . and he will be filled with the Holy Spirit from his mother's womb" (Lk 1:13-15).

Zechariah, you were overjoyed to hear the angel continue this promise and prophecy. "Many of the sons of Israel will he bring back to the Lord their God. God himself will go before him, in the spirit and power of Elijah" (Lk 1:16-17).

This was the greatest news you ever heard. You realized that the long-awaited Savior was soon to come and that your very own son would prepare the way for him. No doubt this was the greatest moment of your life. How very much you wanted to believe! Yet you asked yourself: "Is this a dream?"

I am sure that your heart was beating wildly as you thought not only about finally having a son of your own, but about having a son who was especially chosen by God for this world-shaking mission.

FOUR

Zechariah's Plight

"How am I to know this? I am an old man; my wife too is advanced in age." (Lk 1:18)

I know, Zechariah, that you were soon jarred from your jubilation when the impracticality and the unlikelihood of bearing a son at your age dawned on you. You very much wanted to believe. However, the problem you faced seemed insurmountable. Throughout your long married years the Lord did not bless you with a family because your wife was sterile. Moreover, you were both advanced in years.

It seemed impossible ever to have a child this late in life. It was preposterous and presumptive even to think about such a possibility. All these years you lived with disappointment and regret. You had hoped and prayed fervently, but all to no avail. You hesitated to make yourself so vulnerable again. You could not endure disappointment this late in life. It was too painful. The hope which sprang up in your heart died as quickly as it was kindled.

Nevertheless, you did pursue the possibility by asking the angel: "How am I to know this? I am an old man; my wife too is advanced in age" (Lk 1:18).

You did not deliberately doubt what Gabriel had announced to you, nor did you want to be cynical. You were simply frightened at the prospect of being deeply hurt again. Since you did not have a son to follow you in the priesthood, Aaron's lineage in your family would terminate at your death. Many times throughout your life you had been humiliated and persecuted by your peers because you had no son. Your question was a valid one.

You asked for a sign and the angel gave you one. It was more of a sign than a punishment. "But now you will be mute—unable to speak—until the day these things take place, because you have not trusted my words" (Lk 1:20).

Zechariah, when your priestly service was over, you went home. How happy you were to be at home to reflect and relive such a heavenly experience! Joy filled your heart when you discovered that, as the angel had promised, Elizabeth was pregnant. In the midst of all this rejoicing you must have been anxious, since Elizabeth was quite elderly. You did not want anything to happen to her. God was really putting you to the test, asking for your complete trust and confidence in him as you played this vital role in salvation history.

FIVE

Mother at Last

"His wife Elizabeth conceived. She went into seclusion for five months, saying: 'In these days the Lord is acting on my behalf; he has seen fit to remove my reproach among men.'" (Lk 1:24-25)

I feel that I know you, Elizabeth, since the Gospel vividly describes the role you played in the preparation of the mystery of the Incarnation. You were proud of Zechariah and a little excited about this privileged priestly duty. You prayed with him and for him "while the full assembly of people was praying outside at the incense hour."

Were you worried when he did not come out of the sanctuary in due time? As more time elapsed your anxiety must have intensified. Others, too, were getting concerned. "Meanwhile, the people were waiting for Zechariah, wondering at his delay in the temple" (Lk 1:21).

Your initial excitement now turned to near panic when he finally came out and was unable to speak. I can well imagine the frustration you felt when you tried to find out what had happened and why he could not speak.

Yet your delight knew no bounds when you conceived, as Gabriel had promised. For so many years you had suffered greatly because you were childless. During those years you must have seen the raised eyebrows and pointed fingers of your friends and acquaintances as time passed without your starting a family.

Your heart had ached, since there was no son to follow Zechariah in the priesthood. You had felt keenly Zechariah's disappointment at not having a son to succeed him. Perhaps he had never reproached you, but you could see the concern in his eyes. Throughout these many years you did in fact suffer persecution. But all that was over, for the Lord had seen fit to remove your "reproach among men."

Your joy was even greater when you learned that your son would fulfill an important role in salvation history. Although you could not know all the specific details, your pregnancy, in spite of your old age, made you realize that God had some special plan for your unborn son, as the angel had predicted.

As was the custom, you went into confinement for five months. This was a very precious time for you. In seclusion, you could more easily reflect and contemplate the infinite goodness of God and the mystery of his tremendous love. Your grateful heart overflowed with joy as you sang praises and glorified God in the psalms and prayers of your people.

Announcement of the Birth of Jesus

In the sixth month, the angel Gabriel was sent from God to a town of Galilee named Nazareth, to a virgin bethrothed to a man named Joseph, of the house of David. The virgin's name was Mary. Upon arriving, the angel said to her: "Rejoice, O highly favored daughter! The Lord is with you. Blessed are you among women." She was deeply troubled by his words, and wondered what his greeting meant. The angel went on to say to her: "Do not fear, Mary. You have found favor with God. You shall conceive and bear a son and give him the name Jesus. Great will be his dignity and he will be called Son of the Most High. The Lord God will give him the throne of David his father. He will rule over the house of Jacob forever and his reign will be without end."

Mary said to the angel, "How can this be since I do not know man?" The angel answered her: "The Holy Spirit will come upon you and the power of the Most High will overshadow you; hence, the holy offspring to be born will be called Son of God. Know that Elizabeth your kinswoman has conceived a son in her old age; she who was thought to be sterile is now in her sixth month, for nothing is impossible with God."

Mary said: "I am the servant of the Lord. Let it be done to me as you say." With that the angel left her. (Lk 1:26-38)

SIX

Miriyam

"The angel Gabriel was sent from God to a town of Galilee named Nazareth, to a virgin betrothed to a man named Joseph, of the house of David. The virgin's name was Mary." (Lk 1:26-27)

I like to address you as the Blessed Virgin whose name is Mary. That title is very sacred and hallowed to us. We honor, respect, and revere you as the virginal Mother of Jesus. The people in your day did not interpret this appelation in the same way as we do today. According to the culture of your times, a woman was not considered very important in society until she married and bore children. A virgin, unmarried and childless, was practically a nonentity.

However, you are deliberately called a virgin in the Gospel because the author wanted to make the point that God was not using people who were notable and important in the eyes of the world. He always called upon the *anawim*—the humble, simple people—to accomplish his divine designs.

In our time, you are more commonly called just by your name—Mary. That name is very precious to all of us. Many times when I hear someone called Mary, my thoughts go to you. Mary is a beautiful name and it has found a place within our hearts. Yet it was simply and unobtrusively revealed to us at the time of the Annunciation. "The virgin's name was Mary." This is

17

such a brief revelation and a rather ordinary identification for someone who played such a tremendous role in our salvation.

There are many different explanations offered for the exact meaning and significance of your name. The most fitting seems to be that it came from the word "Miriyam" which means "Exalted One." Such a title is most appropriate for you. In your time, names were extremely important. Names were not only a way of identifying a person but also a distinctive mark of the personality or mission of the individual. This is so true in your case. You really are the "Exalted One" even though you said that God "has looked upon his servant in her lowliness" (Lk 1:48). It was your lowliness which made you truly great.

I recall, too, that you have received more impressive salutations than anyone else throughout the pages of the Scriptures. You were called the "highly favored daughter" by the angel (Lk 1:28). Elizabeth greeted you as the "mother of my Lord" (Lk 1:43). The angel called you "blessed among women."

At least six other women named Mary appear in the New Testament, and Mary is a very popular name today. In almost every community and in many families someone has been baptized with the name Mary. That is proof sufficient how dear you are to us and how much we revere and respect you. We admire and love you not solely for the special mission to which you were called but also for the dedicated and devoted manner in which you responded to your vocation. When we hear your name, our hearts swell with pride and gratitude.

SEVEN

Mother of Faith

"The Holy Spirit will come upon you and the power of the Most High will overshadow you; hence the holy offspring to be born will be called Son of God." (Lk 1:35)

Mother of Faith, how much you have taught me by your immediate response in faith and trust to the call of God as revealed to you through the angel Gabriel!

You were asked to fulfill a role which would appear to the average person to be impossible and in fact quite ridiculous. You were asked to become a mother without your child having a natural father. Such an event had never occurred in the annals of human history. Furthermore, you were aware that pregnancy outside of wedlock was by no means tolerated in the culture of your time.

In spite of all these obstacles, you asked only one question of the angel. You were not asking due to hesitation, nor were you seeking reassurance or guarantees. You were simply trying to discern God's will for you more clearly, wondering exactly how God wanted you to fulfill his will. You merely asked: "How can this be since I do not know man?" In other words, you were saying: "I am not married."

The angel's answer clarified the situation for you. "The Holy Spirit will come upon you and the power of the Most High will overshadow you; hence the holy offspring to be born will be called Son of God" (Lk 1:35).

Although much mystery remained in the angel's

explanation, you were willing to accept it. You stepped out in faith. You placed your complete trust and confidence in God.

There are different levels of faith. Sometimes we may accept a truth or mystery we cannot understand. This acceptance occurs on the intellectual level. Then there is a second degree of faith, the faith of commitment. On this level, we are so convinced about a truth that we are willing to do something about it. We are willing to contribute our time and talent to its fulfillment. Third, there is the level of faith which you manifested so graciously: the faith of expectancy. With this degree of faith, we are certain that God will and does act in every situation.

Mother Mary, your faith was so deep that you did not hesitate to commit yourself to whatever God wanted of you. You were confident that God would take care of all matters in his own divine way.

During his public ministry, Jesus was always pleased when he found faith and trust in him. I remember him saying: "Everything is possible to a man who trusts" (Mk 9:23). Numerous times Jesus assured those who came to him: "Your faith has saved you."

EIGHT

Mary's Fiat

"I am the servant of the Lord. Let it be done to me as you say." (Lk 1:38)

As I reflect on the events which took place at the time of the Annunciation, Mary, I become more and more aware of the total commitment you made on the spur of the moment, a commitment from which you never wavered throughout your sojourn here on earth.

After you discerned that the message from the angel was authentic and was coming from God, you made an uncompromising commitment to the Lord. Your memorable words have lived on through the centuries: "I am the servant of the Lord. Let it be done to me as you say" (Lk 1:38). We often recall your gracious commitment with a single word, "Fiat"—"Let it be done."

Mary, you were enabled to make this immediate and firm commitment because the Holy Spirit had been operating within you. Your sinlessness enabled him to mold and transform your pure soul into a temple overflowing with the love of God.

Your commitment led you into Egypt, a foreign country. You would have preferred to be at home with your family enjoying and sharing your child with them. On your return from this exile, you willingly accepted the poverty of Nazareth. All too soon, your commitment meant an empty household in Nazareth after Jesus left home to begin his public ministry. Your commitment meant your patient waiting and wondering as the rejection and hatred of Jesus' enemies intensified.

John laconically describes your uncompromising and unconditional commitment on the hill of Calvary. "Near the cross of Jesus there stood his mother" (Jn 19:25). The fact that you were standing is significant. It speaks to me of the total oblation of yourself, along with your Son, to the Father for the salvation of the world.

Your commitment continued into the early days of the church. You joined the disciples in the Upper Room after the Ascension, there to pray fervently for the outpouring of the Holy Spirit upon these chosen pillars of the infant church (Acts 1:12ff).

Today, we need the inspiration and support of your powerful example. There seems to be a tremendous lack of commitment in our time, be it to marriage or to other vocations. There seems to be great emphasis on personal likes and dislikes, on feelings and emotions, and an increasing disregard for what God asks of us or of our responsibility toward others.

NINE

Love Must Give

"Rejoice, O highly favored daughter! The Lord is with you." (Lk 1:28)

Mary, what was the secret power underlying your total and unquestioning willingness to cooperate with whatever God asked of you? Your *Fiat* was loud and clear, and you never turned back on your total commitment. So it is quite evident that there was a motivating force enabling you to give yourself so completely to the Lord. This motivating power was your great love for God.

You could give yourself so lovingly to the Lord because of your sinlessness. The fruits of the redemption were applied to you beforehand so that you came into this world free from any sin. Through God's divine dispensation you were able to keep your soul unsoiled by any deliberate sin. Consequently, you were an ideal temple of the Holy Spirit from the first moment of your conception. His divine power was within you, making you able to overcome the fear, insecurity, and selfishness which we daily encounter.

This is why the angel addressed you with those memorable words: "Rejoice, O highly favored daughter! The Lord is with you. Blessed are you among women" (Lk 1:28).

The Holy Spirit is the very essence of divine love. As St. Paul reminds us: "The love of God has been poured out in our hearts through the Holy Spirit who has been given to us" (Rom 5:5).

Love always wants to give and therefore must be translated into action. Mary, you were always eager and anxious to give yourself without reservation to the Lord's plan because your heart overflowed with love for him. Living out the will of God in your life was not a burden for you because of this great love.

Your Son also gives us a compelling example. He was always solicitous about doing the Father's will. For him, obedience was not following orders, but a way and means of making his love-offering to the Father. When we love a person unselfishly, we want to do everything to please that person. Jesus' love for the Father was infinite; hence doing the Father's will was an ideal way of expressing his love.

Jesus encouraged us to commit ourselves in love as he did. Speaking of his supreme act of love, he told us: "The Father loves me for this: / that I lay down my life / to take it up again" (Jn 10:17). Later, he confirmed his love for us: "There is no greater love than this: / to lay down one's life for one's friends" (Jn 15:13). This commitment was by no means an easy one for Jesus. Listen to his agonizing decision: "Father, if it is your will, take this cup from me; yet not my will but yours be done" (Lk 22:42). Jesus made his final love-offering on the cross with these words: "Father, into your hands I commend my spirit" (Lk 23:46).

The Visit

Thereupon Mary set out, proceeding in haste into the hill country to a town of Judah, where she entered Zechariah's house and greeted Elizabeth. When Elizabeth heard Mary's greeting, the baby leapt in her womb. Elizabeth was filled with the Holy Spirit and cried out in a loud voice: "Blest are you among women and blest is the fruit of your womb. But who am I that the mother of my Lord should come to me? The moment your greeting sounded in my ears, the baby leapt in my womb for joy. Blest is she who trusted that the Lord's words to her would be fulfilled." (Lk 1:39-45)

TEN

John Meets Jesus

"Mary set out, proceeding in haste into the hill country to a town of Judah, where she entered Zechariah's house and greeted Elizabeth." (Lk 1:39-40)

Mary, I wonder what your thoughts were as you set out into the hill country to visit your kinswoman Elizabeth. You may have had some misgivings about making such an arduous journey. It required many days of travel, much of it probably on foot. Were you concerned about your physical condition since you were expecting a child?

Your home and background was quite different from that of Elizabeth and Zechariah. Not only were you a poor woman, but you were also coming from the back-country of Galilee. Many of your people considered the Galileans non-practicing Jews because they were unable to make the journey to the temple to worship and participate in all the feasts of the year.

There could have been an additional obstacle. Elizabeth belonged to the priestly class, those Jews who were considered the wealthy class and the socially elite. Did you wonder if you would feel comfortable in the home of Elizabeth and Zechariah?

If such thoughts did occur to you, you quickly expelled them since you and Elizabeth had something in common which far exceeded any of these mundane considerations. Both of you had experienced the power and love of God to be operative in your lives. Furthermore, you were drawn by the Holy Spirit to make this journey to share with Elizabeth. All else was relatively unimportant.

The secret which both of you shared would not only change the world but heaven, too. No wonder, then, that you "set out, proceeding in haste into the hill country to a town of Judah," where you "entered Zechariah's house and greeted Elizabeth" (Lk 1:39-40). Not even your tired feet and aching limbs could prevent you from proceeding in haste.

Mary, Jesus was present within you on your journey by the overshadowing of the Holy Spirit. Even as you carried Jesus in your womb, he was already reaching out to others. In every sense of the word, you are truly a Christopher, bringing Jesus to John. Your journey was important and meaningful to you and to Elizabeth. However, there is even greater significance in this meeting in Zechariah's home. You brought Jesus to encounter John and to confirm him in his vocation. Even though as yet unborn physically, Jesus brought his Holy Spirit to his precursor. Elizabeth recognized that the power of God was alive in her unborn child. Her memorable words are the key to the importance of this meeting. "The moment your greeting sounded in my ears, the baby leapt in my womb for joy" (Lk 1:44). John was responding to the presence of Jesus. It is commonly believed that at this moment Jesus, the Incarnate Word, sanctified John. Thus the first grace was poured out through you, Mary.

For his part Jesus was commissioning John to inaugurate and "Make ready the way of the Lord, /

Clear him a straight path. / . . . and all mankind shall
see the salvation of God" (Lk 3:4-6).

ELEVEN

Elizabeth's Devotion

"Who am I that the mother of my Lord should come to me?"
(Lk 1:43)

In Hebrew, Elizabeth means "worshiper of God."
Your name fits you perfectly. You were one of the first
to acknowledge Jesus and to greet Mary as "the
mother of my Lord" (Lk 1:43).

I am curious—were you aware that Mary was
enroute to visit you, or was her arrival a complete
surprise? The Holy Spirit had already endowed you
with many inspirations and insights; therefore, you
could have known Mary's secret as well as your own.

From a human standpoint, I can imagine that there
might have been a tinge of envy or even resentment in
your heart because Mary was pregnant at such an early
age. After all, for so many years you knew only
frustration and disappointment, having little or no
hope of ever bearing a family.

If any such feelings ever did surface, they were gone
once you became aware that God was working
powerfully in your life and that your pregnancy was
surely miraculous. How convincingly God spoke to
you when your unborn son recognized the long-
awaited Messiah. John was so delighted that he leaped

with joy in your womb. How proud you must have been to bear a son who would fulfill such an essential role in God's plan of salvation.

You were docile to the Holy Spirit as he filled you and inspired you to cry out in a loud voice when you recognized Mary to be chosen by God for a special ministry. "Who am I that the mother of my Lord should come to me?" (Lk 1:43). Elizabeth, you were the very first to call Mary the Mother of God, a title which she has borne throughout all Christian times.

Your crying out in a loud voice gives evidence of the ecstatic joy which filled your heart and Mary's as you shared the love and power of God operative within you. Neither humanness, pettiness, nor the hurts of the past could interfere with your personal relationship with God and with each other. Only the Lord could establish such a holy bond between two people. Little wonder that Mary burst forth with her jubilant hymn of praise and prophecy.

Zechariah could not communicate verbally with you, but his eyes and heart danced with joy. All his hopes and expectations of the past were being fulfilled before his very eyes. Those expectations not only concerned his own family but also all of Israel "because he (God) has visited and ransomed his people" (Lk 1:68).

Mary had come to share her joy with you. Your home was sanctified, for she brought the Lord with her. Truly, your home was the vestibule of heaven. Throughout the three months of Mary's sojourn, joy reigned supreme in your home as you celebrated the goodness of the Lord.

TWELVE

Blest among Women

"Blest are you among women and blest is the fruit of your womb." (Lk 1:42)

Elizabeth, I am deeply grateful to you for many reasons. In the first place, you acquiesced to God's designs for you and your chosen son. In this way you played an important role in bringing about our redemption. I am only one of many down through the ages who enjoy the resulting fruit of God's saving power.

The words of the prophet Isaiah aptly apply to your son, John. "The Lord called me from birth, / from my mother's womb he gave me my name" (Is 49:1). When God gives someone a special name or changes a person's name, he is designating that person for a special office. How true this proved in the case of your son, whose name was given by the angel who appeared to Zechariah in the temple at the incense hour. Thank you for your devoted spirit of cooperation with God's designs.

You have led countless people into a more prayerful relationship with the Lord through the intercession of Mary. One of the first formal prayers I learned at my mother's knee was the Hail Mary. Many years later I discovered that the words with which you greeted Mary under the inspiration of the Holy Spirit contributed much to this popular prayer.

You were receptive to the enlightenment of the Holy

Spirit, which enabled you not only to recognize Mary's blessedness but also to give testimony of it to the world. Your words, "Blest are you among women and blest is the fruit of your womb," are an essential part of the Hail Mary. Your acknowledgment of Mary's blessedness helps me to appreciate her unique role in God's design. It also increases my admiration for Mary, my Mother and the Mother of Jesus. Thank you for helping me be more prayerful.

Elizabeth, you also recognized Mary's faith. You praised her for her vibrant, dynamic faith which enabled her to give her "fiat" to the Lord without reservation. Your statement is brief but it means much. "Blest is she who trusted that the Lord's words to her would be fulfilled" (Lk 1:45). These memorable words of yours are not incorporated in the Hail Mary, but they live in my heart and strengthen my faltering faith on many occasions.

Mary's Heart Sings

Then Mary said:
"My being proclaims the greatness of the Lord,
*   my spirit finds joy in God my savior,*
For he has looked upon his servant in her lowliness;
*   all ages to come shall call me blessed.*
God who is mighty has done great things for me,
*   holy is his name:*
His mercy is from age to age
*   on those who fear him.*
He has shown might with his arm;
he has confused the proud in their inmost thoughts.
He has deposed the mighty from their thrones
*   and raised the lowly to high places.*
The hungry he has given every good thing,
*   while the rich he has sent empty away.*
He has upheld Israel his servant,
*   ever mindful of his mercy;*
Even as he promised our fathers,
*   promised Abraham and his descendants forever."*

Mary remained with Elizabeth about three months and
then returned home. (Lk 1: 46-56)

THIRTEEN

My Spirit Finds Joy

"My being proclaims the greatness of the Lord, / my spirit finds joy in God my savior, / For he has looked upon his servant in her lowliness; / all ages to come shall call me blessed." (Lk 1:46-48)

As you and Elizabeth experienced the deep inner joy of God's mysterious love at work in both of you, your heart naturally overflowed with this memorable hymn popularly called the Magnificat. Mary, your prayer of praise and thanksgiving to God has echoed down through the ages to become the daily prayer of the church.

There are certain sentiments of the heart which cannot be expressed in words. There never have been, nor will there ever be, words capable of voicing the deepest feelings within us. When we strive to speak about God, words seem so hollow and empty. At such times, our hearts want to burst forth in songs and hymns of praise. You and Elizabeth shared some rich experiences of God, and your hearts wanted to sing out with joy and exultation.

Your canticle reflects the prayerfulness of your whole being. Mary, you spent long hours meditating and contemplating all the wonderful deeds of the Lord throughout the history of the chosen people. You were well acquainted with the extravagant goodness of God as recorded throughout the Hebrew Testament. You arranged these words of Scripture with your own reflections on them and created a beautiful mosaic portraying God's love for his people.

As you journeyed from your home in Nazareth to visit Elizabeth, you spent the long, weary days of travel pondering God's mysterious love which was operative in these events of salvation history. Your prayerfulness is evident in this beautiful hymn praising and glorifying God for his wondrous love.

Mary, you are truly a humble person. Your humility is reflected in the words of the Magnificat. In your humility you recognized that God called you to a very privileged office, but you acknowledged that it was not due to your own merits. Thus you prayed: "God who is mighty has done great things for me, / holy is his name" (Lk 1:49).

Genuine humility is the truth. It is the truth of the power and might of God, and the truth of our own helplessness without him. Jesus said: "Apart from me you can do nothing" (Jn 15:5). True humility makes us aware that we can accomplish nothing by ourselves, but with God's help we can do many things, some of which seem almost impossible. We must be as clay in the potter's hand so that he can mold and transform us. Because of your lowliness, Mary, God transformed you into the kind of person he wanted you to be as the Mother of his Son.

FOURTEEN
Mary's Prophetic Prayer

"His mercy is from age to age / on those who fear him. / He has shown might with his arm; / he has confused the proud in their inmost thoughts." (Lk 1:50-51)

Mary, your words recorded in Scripture are so few that it never occurred to me to think of you as a prophetess until I spent more time reflecting on the thoughts you expressed in the Magnificat. In this prayer, I find at least four prophetic pronouncements which really arrested my attention.

You recall God's dealings with his people in the past, giving us assurance that Jesus would implement and fulfill those promises in the way of life he would present to his followers. You assure us that "His mercy is from age to age on those who fear him." God had always been a merciful, compassionate Father to those who reverenced and worshiped him. You promise us in addition that the redemptive love of Jesus will always be with us if we remain receptive to his forgiving, healing, redeeming love.

Your second prophecy is, "He has shown might with his arm; / he has confused the proud in their inmost thoughts." In the Old Testament times, God did humble the proud. Jesus continues to emphasize the need for humility when he says: "Everyone who exalts himself shall be humbled and he who humbles himself shall be exalted" (Lk 14:11). The act of following in the footsteps of Jesus, and striving to live as he did, will deal a death blow to our pride.

The third phase of your prophecy followed, as you said: "He has deposed the mighty from their thrones / and raised the lowly to high places" (Lk 1:52). Mary, you were trying to tell us that God has no favorites. Like his Father, Jesus would treat everyone alike because he loves every person with an infinite, immutable love. Some years later Jesus would reiterate his boundless love. "As the Father has loved me, / so I have loved you" (Jn 15:9). In his kingdom there are no privileged people, no labels, no prestige. We are all the adopted sons and daughters of the Father.

You continued: "The hungry he has given every good thing, / while the rich he has sent empty away." I am sure that you were speaking about spiritual hunger. Jesus himself said: "No one who comes to me shall ever be hungry, / no one who believes in me shall ever thirst" (Jn 6:35). There is a longing and a restlessness in every human heart which only Jesus can satisfy. Only in him will we find peace. This is what you were trying to tell us.

Divine Intervention

Now this is how the birth of Jesus Christ came about. When his mother Mary was engaged to Joseph, but before they lived together, she was found with child through the power of the Holy Spirit. Joseph her husband, an upright man unwilling to expose her to the law, decided to divorce her quietly. Such was his intention when suddenly the angel of the Lord appeared in a dream and said to him: "Joseph, son of David, have no fear about taking Mary as your wife. It is by the Holy Spirit that she has conceived this child. She is to have a son and you are to name him Jesus because he will save his people from their sins." All this happened to fulfill what the Lord had said through the prophet:

"The virgin shall be with child
and give birth to a son,
and they shall call him Emmanuel,
a name which means "God is with us."

When Joseph awoke he did as the angel of the Lord had directed him and received her into his home as his wife. He had no relations with her at any time before she bore a son, whom he named Jesus. (Mt 1:18-25)

FIFTEEN

Joseph, an Upright Man

"When his mother Mary was engaged to Joseph, but before they lived together, she was found with child through the power of the Holy Spirit. Joseph her husband, an upright man unwilling to expose her to the law, decided to divorce her quietly." (Mt 1:18-20)

Joseph, Scripture pays you a very high tribute when it tells us that you were an "upright man." That implies that you were the epitome of all goodness and holiness.

Even though you were a good man, you were chagrined and perplexed when you discovered that Mary was pregnant. Since you loved her so dearly you were "unwilling to expose her to the law" and you "decided to divorce her quietly." According to the law and custom of that day, you had no choice.

Who of us can imagine the pain which you felt? During your sleepless nights, you probably cried out: "Why, Lord? How could this happen?" In your waking hours your heart was heavy and your feet leaden as you went about your daily duties. You were deeply hurt because you loved Mary with an overwhelming love.

When Mary saw the pain and disappointment in your eyes, she too suffered the sharp pains of sorrow. How could she explain the mysterious workings of God in her life? Even if she could explain, how could she expect you to understand? None of us can explain

41

in human terms, nor can we comprehend with our finite minds, the towering plans of God, nor the profound mysteries of his designs in our world.

What a gracious blessing "when suddenly the angel of the Lord appeared in a dream and said to him: 'Joseph, son of David, have no fear about taking Mary as your wife. It is by the Holy Spirit that she has conceived this child. She is to have a son and you are to name him Jesus because he will save his people from their sins'" (Mt 1:20-21). What Good News for you and for the whole world. Although you did not fully understand the meaning of the angel's message, you probably said, like the rest of us must say from time to time: "I do believe, Lord, help my unbelief."

The words of the prophet possibly came to mind: "I know well the plans I have in mind for you, says the Lord, plans for your welfare, not for woe! plans to give you a future full of hope" (Jer 29:11).

SIXTEEN

Joseph, Man of Great Faith

"Suddenly the angel of the Lord appeared in a dream and said to him: Joseph, son of David, have no fear about taking Mary as your wife. It is by the Holy Spirit that she has conceived this child.'" (Mt 1:20)

Joseph, by understanding the culture of your time, I can see why you thought you had no other alternative but to divorce Mary. Engagements in your day were made very early in life, either by the parents or by a professional matchmaker. When the young people grew up, the engagement could either be ratified by the betrothal or broken off. The betrothal lasted for one year before the marriage could take place. After the betrothal had taken place, it could be broken only by a divorce.

Your thoughtfulness, kindness, and gracious consideration radiate throughout this situation. You could rightfully have divorced Mary publicly, but this would have caused much scandal and embarrassment to her and her family. How gracious of you to consider divorcing her privately, without exposing her to the law.

I wonder how I would have reacted. I constantly sit in judgment on others on the least provocation. My critical remarks frequently expose the faults of another person in order to justify and defend myself.

As a practicing Jew, you believed in the Holy Spirit although you did not yet have any clear ideas about the Holy Trinity. As a good Jew, you believed that the Holy Spirit brought God's truth to men and helped them recognize the truth as coming from God. That is why you did not hesitate to accept the message of your dream when the angel appeared to you and told you of the source of Mary's pregnancy.

Joseph, you were a man of great faith to believe that Mary conceived by the power of the Holy Spirit. You were humble enough to accept the angel's message without additional proof. You asked for no further confirmation. This required a strong faith because you were so personally involved and so painfully hurt when you first discovered Mary's condition.

A Prophet Is Born

When Elizabeth's time for delivery arrived, she gave birth to a son. Her neighbors and relatives, upon hearing that the Lord had extended his mercy to her, rejoiced with her. When they assembled for the circumcision of the child on the eighth day, they intended to name him after his father Zechariah. At this his mother intervened, saying, "No, he is to be called John."

They pointed out to her, "None of your relatives has this name." Then, using signs, they asked the father what he wished him to be called.

He signaled for a writing tablet and wrote the words, "His name is John." This astonished them all. At that moment his mouth was opened and his tongue loosed, and he began to speak in praise of God.

Fear descended on all in the neighborhood; throughout the hill country of Judea these happenings began to be recounted to the last detail. All who heard stored these things up in their hearts, saying, "What will this child be?" and, "Was not the hand of the Lord upon him?" (Lk 1:57-66)

SEVENTEEN

Zechariah and Elizabeth

"When Elizabeth's time for delivery arrived, she gave birth to a son. Her neighbors and relatives, upon hearing that the Lord had extended his mercy to her, rejoiced with her." (Lk 1:57-58)

I must join your "neighbors and relatives," Zechariah and Elizabeth, in congratulating you and rejoicing with you on this blessed event in your lives. The birth of a child is always a time for celebration and rejoicing. Life is a precious gift from God. Such a celebration is not only a joyous welcome to the child but also a way of manifesting our gratitude and reverence to our creating Father for the gift of life which extends throughout eternity.

You had many reasons for rejoicing. John was God's gift to you after many lonely years of waiting. He was the living proof of God's fidelity to his promises. God is always faithful.

It must have seemed an eternity to you from the day the angel appeared to you as you were offering incense in the sanctuary, until the day of John's birth months later. During those days of anticipation, you probably reflected many times on how favored you were. You knew you were chosen by God to bear a son who would fulfill such an important prophetic role in the salvation of all people. Zechariah and Elizabeth, you yourselves were precious to God, and that is why he chose you to be the parents of his great prophet.

Finally the happy day came. I can well imagine the

enthusiasm with which the musicians struck up their instruments when they learned that a son had been born to you. Your custom of serenading and welcoming a newborn child was a pleasant one.

The music and the rejoicing of the neighbors and relatives brought tears to your eyes. Your hearts overflowed with gratitude for the goodness of God to you in your old age. The angel promised that it would be a happy occassion when he told you: "Joy and gladness will be yours, and many will rejoice at his birth" (Lk 1:14).

There was an even greater reason for your happiness. God had some unique plans for your son, John. He was being called to an extraordinary mission in life. The angel brought you the message that "Many of the sons of Israel will he bring back to the Lord their God," and he will "prepare for the Lord a people well-disposed" (Lk 1:16f).

As I contemplate this event in your life, I am deeply impressed by the vibrant faith with which you accepted all the promises and prophecies concerning the birth of John. You had great confidence and trust in God. There were many unnatural circumstances surrounding all that was taking place. You discerned rightly that there was a supernatural power at work.

EIGHTEEN

His Name Is John

" 'No, he is to be called John.' . . . 'His name is John.'" (Lk 1:60, 63)

I would have stood up and shouted with joy, Zechariah, when you "signaled for a writing tablet and wrote the words, 'His name is John.'" I am sure that you wrote those words with a firm hand and visible determination. Elizabeth, you, too, were adamant when everyone wanted you to name him after his father Zechariah. How resolutely you said: "No, he is to be called John."

At that time, writing required some effort. The ordinary writing material was a piece of wood painted or stained dark and covered with wax. Writing was done with a metal stylus. The tablet could easily be erased and used over and over again.

Both of you were determined to carry out precisely the events that God had revealed to you through the angel. "Your wife Elizabeth shall bear a son whom you shall name John" (Lk 1:13). Elizabeth, how did you know that he should be called John? Was this a special inspiration of the Holy Spirit, or did Zechariah somehow convey to you the request of the angel even though he was mute?

Zechariah, as the father of John your decision was final. According to the custom of your time, the ceremony of the father's naming the child was extremely important. It was an expression of the father's willingness to love, to provide for, and to educate the child—in other words, to take the full responsibility for caring for the child.

In Israel, names were descriptive. They might describe something about the child: Laban, for instance, meant white or blond. Names might also say something about the parents—for example, their faith or dedication to God. The name Saul or Samuel described the parents' joy.

John is a meaningful name. It is a short form of "Jehohanan" which means "Yahweh's gift" or "God is gracious." Besides being a name requested by God, the name John also expressed your gratefulness to God for this unexpected joy.

Zechariah, as soon as you complied with God's will in naming the child, your gift of speech was restored. Naturally you "began to speak in praise of God" (Lk 1:64). Your friends and neighbors were filled with awe and reverence when they beheld God's wonderful deeds in your lives. They were obviously aware of the deeper meaning of these unusual events. The whole countryside marveled and wondered what would happen next.

Zechariah and Elizabeth, both of you must have smiled within yourselves when people asked: "'What will this child be?'" and "'Was not the hand of the Lord upon him?'" (Lk 1:66). You prayed that your son would succeed in the great mission to which God had called him.

John carried out his apostolate perfectly. During his contemplative years in the desert he was molded and transformed into a fearless preacher of the Good News, telling others to prepare for the coming of the Messiah through prayer and reformation of life. John did so with such zeal that he earned the martyr's crown.

A Father's
Prophetic Hymn of Praise

*Then Zechariah his father, filled with the Holy Spirit,
uttered this prophecy:*

*"Blessed be the Lord the God of Israel
    because he has visited and ransomed his people.
He has raised a horn of saving strength for us
    in the house of David his servant.
As he promised through the mouths of his holy ones,
    the prophets of ancient times:
Salvation from our enemies
    and from the hands of all our foes.
He has dealt mercifully with our fathers
    and remembered the holy covenant he made.
The oath he swore to Abraham our father he would grant
    us:
    that, rid of fear and delivered from the enemy,
We should serve him devoutly and through all our days
    be holy in his sight.
And you, O child, shall be called
    prophet of the Most High;
For you shall go before the Lord
    to prepare straight paths for him,
Giving his people a knowledge of salvation
    in freedom from their sins.
All this is the work of the kindness of our God:
    he, the Dayspring, shall visit us in his mercy*

To shine on those who sit in darkness and in the shadow of death,
  to guide our feet into the way of peace."

The child grew up and matured in spirit. He lived in the desert until the day when he made his public appearance in Israel. (Lk 1:67-80)

NINETEEN

Zechariah, Teacher and Interpreter

"Blessed be the Lord the God of Israel / because he has visited and ransomed his people. / He has raised a horn of saving strength for us / in the house of David his servant." (Lk 1:68-69)

Zechariah, I am delighted that the church has incorporated your prayerful canticle into her liturgical prayer. Each time I pray with the words you gave us, I can imagine the sheer joy which filled your heart as you sang this glorious hymn of praise.

Like the psalmist of old, you experienced the power and presence of the Lord in your life. Now your heart and voice sing his praises and predict his saving acts yet to come. You performed a masterful task in composing this hymn of praise. Under the inspiration of the Holy Spirit, you cleverly wove many of the Old Testament's thoughts and themes, promises and prophecies into this sublime prayer.

Your hymn is genuinely prophetic. Enlightened by divine inspiration, you shared your great vision of the Messiah's "saving strength" and the ransoming of his people. Your prophecy recalls for us the promises of "the prophets of ancient times" (Lk 1:70) in order to prepare us for the salvation which Jesus will soon bring us.

I understand that a prophet does not simply foretell future events but also proclaims and interprets the meaning of God's acting in our lives. A prophet is also a teacher. This is precisely how you fulfilled your prophetic mission.

In the first part of your hymn of praise and thanksgiving, you prepared your own people for the coming of the Lord as Savior and Redeemer. Our way must lead us to Jesus the Messiah, who in turn leads us to the Father. Your hymn made the people of your own day ready for the saving mission of Jesus, and it continues even today to make us receptive to his presence and power in our lives.

Zechariah, I am grateful to you for teaching us so much about our relationship with God our Father. You informed us that God "dealt mercifully with our fathers / and remembered the holy covenant he made" (Lk 1:72). Many people of your day regarded God as a demanding, exacting lawgiver and judge. Your words assured them, as they assure us, that he is a loving God who calls all of us to salvation. In fact, he wants our eternal happiness more than we could want it ourselves. Your prayer recalls the prophecies which foretold his saving love. You assured your people and you assure us that the fulfillment of these prophecies is about to take place in an even greater measure, as the Messiah will soon enter the world.

We did not know very much about the Father until Jesus came to reveal more about him to us. In this prayer, you tried to share your own broader vision of the Father with us. In your prophetic message, you underscored the mercy and forgiveness of the Lord, emphasizing the fact that he had dealt mercifully in the past. Jesus corroborates your teaching and assures us that his mercy will continue in ever greater abundance if we are open to receive it.

TWENTY

The Prophet Zechariah

"And you, O child, shall be called / prophet of the Most High; / For you shall go before the Lord / to prepare straight paths for him." (Lk 1:76)

In the second portion of your prophetic hymn of praise, Zechariah, you turn your attention to your own son, John, and what he is called to be and to do for the Lord. It was revealed to you that John would be a great prophet and the one to prepare the way for the coming of the Messiah. You understood that he would come in the spirit of Elijah to "'make ready the way of the Lord'" and "'clear him a straight path'" (Lk 3:4). You said: "You, O child, shall be called / prophet of the Most High."

John's prophetic role is a vital link between the promises and prophecies of the Old Testament and the immediate preparation for their fulfillment in Christian times. In fact, John played a singular part in terminating the promises and prophecies of the Old Testament and inaugurating the prophetic role in the New Testament era.

In your prophetic vision, you foresaw that John would prepare the people for the coming of the Messiah by "giving his people a knowledge of salvation / in freedom from their sins" (Lk 1:77). John carried out that injunction, for "he went about the entire region of the Jordan proclaiming a baptism of repentance which led to the forgiveness of sins" (Lk 3:3).

When the people heard John's message and experienced the hope and peace which it engendered in their hearts, they suspected that he might be the Messiah himself. John was quick to correct them. He identified himself to the crowd by declaring: "I am 'a voice in the desert, crying out: / Make straight the way of the Lord'" (Jn 1:23).

Zechariah, your prophecies were authentic as is evidenced by the proclamations which fulfilled your predictions. Scripture relates it in these words: "When John the Baptizer made his appearance as a preacher in the desert of Judea, this was his theme: 'Reform your lives! The reign of God is at hand'" (Mt 3:1-2).

When John was no longer able to preach because of his arrest, Jesus himself preached the same message, again in fulfillment of your prophecy. "After John's arrest, Jesus appeared in Galilee proclaiming the good news of God: 'This is the time of fulfillment. The reign of God is at hand! Reform your lives and believe in the gospel!'" (Mk 1:14f).

Nor did the message stop with Jesus. At his very first recorded sermon Peter was asked: "'What are we to do, brothers?' Peter answered: 'You must reform and be baptized, each one of you, in the name of Jesus Christ, that your sins may be forgiven; then you will receive the gift of the Holy Spirit'" (Acts 2:38).

TWENTY-ONE

Zechariah Points Out the Way of Peace

"To shine on those who sit in darkness and in the shadow of death, / to guide our feet into the way of peace." (Lk 1:79)

The closing words of your famous canticle bring me a great deal of comfort and consolation. Zechariah, you point out that peace would be the special gift which the Messiah would bring, that he will "guide our feet into the way of peace."

The word which you used for peace was the word "*shalom.*" This Hebrew word has a richer, fuller meaning than our word "peace." *Shalom* does not merely mean freedom from troubles; it asks for the highest good which God wants for all of us—salvation. At the birth of Jesus, which would occur not too long after that of John, the angels informed us that Jesus as Savior would bring "peace on earth to those on whom his favor rests" (Lk 2:14).

Your son John preached a reformation of life and a baptism of repentance which is the source of genuine peace. He guided our feet to Jesus who gained this precious gift for us.

Your hymn brought hope to those who were awaiting a Redeemer. The darkness of sin had enveloped the world, and spiritual death was imminent for many. When everything seems darkest, then, as you promised, God sends hope. The birth of John, the precursor of the Messiah, enkindled hope anew in the heart of all people.

At the Last Supper the night before he died, Jesus promised that his redemptive death would be the source of our peace. He said: "'Peace' is my farewell to you, / my peace is my gift to you; / I do not give it to you as the world gives peace" (Jn 14:27).

Birth of Jesus

In those days Caesar Augustus published a decree ordering a census of the whole world. This first census took place while Quirinius was governor of Syria. Everyone went to register, each to his own town. And so Joseph went from the town of Nazareth in Galilee to Judea, to David's town of Bethlehem—because he was of the house and lineage of David—to register with Mary, his espoused wife, who was with child.

While they were there the days of her confinement were completed. She gave birth to her first-born son and wrapped him in swaddling clothes and laid him in a manger, because there was no room for them in the place where travelers lodged. (Lk 2:1-7)

TWENTY-TWO

Mary and Joseph Obey the Decree

Joseph went from the town of Nazareth in Galilee to Judea,
to David's town of Bethlehem—because he was of the house
and lineage of David—to register with Mary, his espoused
wife, who was with child. (Lk 2:4-5)

You were law-abiding people who complied with the
decrees that went forth that all citizens must go to
their ancestral homes to be enrolled. Mary, your
physical condition might have warranted your asking
for an exemption, but you did not do so.

This census had a definite purpose. The Romans
occupying your country wanted to know the number
of potential taxpayers so that they could levy the
maximum amount of taxation in order to enrich
themselves. In other countries, the census had a dual
purpose. It was also taken to ascertain the number of
men eligible for military service. Fortunately, through
God's providence your country was spared that pro-
scription.

How tragic that you could find no hospitality in
Bethlehem but had to take refuge in what was probably
a dark, dismal hovel. Yet it was all aglow.

Mary, as your first-born rested in the embrace of
your loving arms, your countenance radiated a profound inner peace and joy which illumined the whole
setting.

Joseph, your own exuberance over the fact that you
had finally found shelter further helped to light up a

scene that might otherwise have been dark and dreary.

Yet the real source of light was that Jesus came as the Light of the World. His presence in this crude shelter made the difference.

The world at that time, as now, was dark and dreary, steeped in sin. Jesus came as the Light of the World and a tremendous transformation took place. He brought hope and great expectation. We live with that same hope and expectation today.

Jesus also gave us the assurance that he came to light the way for all of us to lead us back to the Father in our heavenly home. I often recall his words: "I am the light of the world. / No follower of mine shall ever walk in darkness; / no, he shall possess the light of life" (Jn 8:12).

He came to share his life and light with us so that we, in turn, may bring light to others. "You are the light of the world," he told us. "Your light must shine before men so that they may see goodness in your acts and give praise to your heavenly Father" (Mt 5:14, 16). It all started in Bethlehem.

TWENTY-THREE

No Room at the Inn for the Holy Family

"She [Mary] gave birth to her first-born son and wrapped him in swaddling clothes and laid him in a manger, because there was no room for them in the place where travelers lodged." (Lk 2:7)

I am always distraught when I read the words, "There was no room for them in the place where travelers lodged." The inn was by no means elegant. It was a walled-in enclosure with no roof. People stayed in the little porticos around the perimeter while animals were kept in the center area where there was usually a well supplying water for domestic use and for the animals. This area would certainly not have provided the privacy which you, Mary, deserved.

The owner did not know you, nor could he suspect who your offspring might be, but his heart should have softened when he saw your physical condition, or when he learned how many days you had been on the road, traveling some ninety miles from Nazareth. Perhaps you were victims of discrimination when he perceived that you were poor. Be that as it may, you were denied hospitality. However, God had other plans for you.

How discouraging this was for you, Joseph. How heavy your heart must have been as you were turned away. It was probably getting quite late; opportunities for finding shelter were few. It was a blow to your fatherly inclination to protect and provide for your loved ones. Did your faith in human nature waver?

"No room for him in the inn" was a foreshadowing of the attitude towards Jesus during his public ministry. He sought entry into the closed and stony hearts of his own people as he traversed the streets and lanes of his homeland. The only place that there was room for him was on the cross. No one denied him that space.

That sad commentary is equally true in our times. Today Jesus continues to seek reception into the hearts of men and women throughout the world, but there is little room in our over-crowded hearts. Many of us are so preoccupied with our pursuit of trivia that we have neither the time nor the inclination to welcome the Lord into our lives.

Far more tragic is the fact that many have usurped certain rights which belong to God alone. Many people today have decided that there is no room for countless unborn babies. Their rejection carries with it great finality, as daily the lives of helpless children are snuffed out. There is no room for them in our stony hearts.

In spite of these constant and frequent rejections, Jesus continues his search. If we listen at the depth of our being, we can hear his invitation: "Come to me, all you who are weary and find life burdensome, and I will refresh you" (Mt 11:28).

TWENTY-FOUR

Mary's Silent Adoration

"While they were there the days of her confinement were completed. She gave birth to her first-born son and wrapped him in swaddling clothes and laid him in a manger." (Lk. 2:6-7)

Mary, the Incarnation is beyond doubt the most profound condescension on the part of God. Your contemplative attitude draws me into a posture of awe, wonder, and reverence.

God came into the world in the person of Jesus to salvage a race steeped in sin. The compassionate Father's response to our sinfulness was the gift of Jesus who became like us in everything except sin in order to redeem us. "Yes, God so loved the world [and me] / that he gave us his only Son" (Jn 3:16).

Surely this superabundance of love is a mystery which we cannot comprehend. The only explanation we can imagine is that God's love for us is absolutely infinite. Furthermore, Jesus came into the world as a helpless, vulnerable, homeless child born in dire poverty. In this, too, God had a specific purpose. Jesus came as a child to win us not by political or military might but by the power of his love. Love is the most motivating and powerful force in the world.

At the time of his coming many were deeply disappointed. They were expecting a mighty monarch, a fearless warrior, or an earth-shaking act of God, to deliver them from the hand of Rome and make them a world power.

Mary, how different was your attitude and expectation. Most of the Christmas cards I receive picture you kneeling at the manger in silent adoration. Your eyes gaze tenderly upon your infant Son. Your posture is the key to my understanding the brevity, the simplicity, of the Gospel account of the birth of Jesus.

Mary, my Mother, your contemplative posture shows that you understood the mystery and the love which prompted God's incomprehensible condescension. St. Paul also had insight into this mystery when he wrote: "He emptied himself / and took the form of a slave, / being born in the likeness of men" (Phil 2:7).

This is such a tremendous mystery that there never has been, nor will there ever be, words capable of describing the magnitude of God's unconditional love.

TWENTY-FIVE

Mary, the Servant of the Lord

"She wrapped him in swaddling clothes and laid him in a manger." (Lk 2:7)

With maternal love and care, Mary, you wrapped Jesus in swaddling clothes and laid him in a manger. The swaddling clothes are symbolic in themselves. The great king Solomon was attired in the same fashion. We read: "In swaddling clothes and with constant care I was nurtured. / For no king has any different origin or birth" (Wis 7:4-5). Is this passage prophetic? Did not the angels refer specifically to this when they announced Jesus' birth to the shepherds? "Let this be a sign to you: in a manger you will find an infant wrapped in swaddling clothes" (Lk 2:12).

You laid Jesus in a manger. That, too, is highly symbolic. The manger was a trough in which the animals were fed. Today, in our creches, we usually use a neat wooden structure to remind us of the manger. However, the manger of your day was probably a hollowed-out rock used for feeding animals.

Mary, not only was your Son Jesus born in poverty but you both spent your entire earthly existence in poverty. Jesus could say of himself: "The foxes have lairs, the birds in the sky have nests, but the Son of Man has nowhere to lay his head" (Mt 8:20). On the cross Jesus was stripped of everything he could call his own. "They took his garments and divided them four ways, one for each soldier" (Jn 19:23). They threw dice to see who would get his seamless robe. Jesus even entrusted you, his dearest possession on earth, to us and to the immediate care of John.

Jesus was born and spent his life in poverty with no earthly possessions in order to teach us detachment from all things which might impede our progress on our journey heavenward.

What is the significance of the manger? Jesus came to nourish and nurture all people with his divine life and love. Since the manger is a hollowed-out rock, it conveys a sense of stability and perpetuity. Jesus continues to feed us daily in all of the sacraments, especially in the Eucharist. In every eucharistic celebration Jesus is born again. He continues to condescend to our needs, making each day another Christmas Day.

Mary, when you placed Jesus in the manger, you offered him not only to the shepherds but to the whole flock, the people of God, the church. Furthermore, this action typified your special role as the "servant of the Lord" (Lk 1:38).

Your action is also a reminder to us that each day is Christmas Day. Jesus becomes Eucharist for us so that we, in turn, may become Eucharist to others. As the Mass draws to a close, the celebrant commissions us to fulfill the same role as you did in becoming the "servant of the Lord." That mission is made explicit in the words: "Go in peace to love and serve the Lord."

The Shepherds

There were shepherds in that region, living in the fields and keeping night watch by turns over their flocks. The angel of the Lord appeared to them as the glory of the Lord shone around them, and they were very much afraid. The angel said to them: "You have nothing to fear! I come to proclaim good news to you—tidings of great joy to be shared by the whole people. This day in David's city a savior has been born to you, the Messiah and Lord. Let this be a sign to you: in a manger you will find an infant wrapped in swaddling clothes." Suddenly, there was with the angel a multitude of the heavenly host, praising God and saying,

"Glory to God in high heaven,
peace on earth to those on whom his favor rests."

When the angels had returned to heaven, the shepherds said to one another: "Let us go over to Bethlehem and see this event which the Lord has made known to us." They went in haste and found Mary and Joseph, and the baby lying in the manger; once they saw, they understood what had been told them concerning this child. All who heard of it were astonished at the report given them by the shepherds.

Mary treasured all these things and reflected on them in her heart. The shepherds returned, glorifying and praising God for all they had heard and seen, in accord with what had been told them. (Lk 2:8-20)

TWENTY-SIX

In the Shepherds' Field

"There were shepherds in that region, living in the fields and keeping night watch by turns over their flocks. The angel of the Lord appeared to them as the glory of the Lord shone around them, and they were very much afraid." (Lk 2:8-9)

I can comprehend to some extent how terrified you must have been on that memorable night in the fields "as the glory of the Lord" shone around you. You had every right to be afraid.

All was quiet and peaceful during the night. After foraging throughout the daylight hours, the sheep were resting quietly. Some of you were asleep while others kept a vigilant eye on the sheep, for you were "living in the fields and keeping night watch by turns over the flocks."

When the presence or power of God is apparent in some event in our own lives, it causes some alarm and fear. When this initial reaction is accompanied by a sense of peace, we usually experience a reverential awe and wonder rather than a paralyzing fear.

Even Mary had to be reassured by the angel at the time of the Annunciation. The angel allayed your fears, too, when he assured you: "You have nothing to fear."

Then you were privileged to be the very first to hear the announcement which would change the face of the earth. "I come to proclaim good news to you—tidings of great joy to be shared by the whole people. This day in David's city a savior has been born to you, the Messiah and Lord."

I am delighted that God chose you to hear and proclaim this world-shaking message. Shepherds were not regarded with much esteem by the law-abiding Jews of the time. In fact, some considered shepherds to be unlearned, uncouth, and unkempt.

The constant care and vigilance which your flocks required prevented you from observing all the minutiae of the Law. You could not participate in the temple worship regularly, nor could you observe the meticulous washing of hands and all the other pro-scriptions of the Law.

Despite this stigma, God chose you. No one is unimportant to God. His love for all of us is un-conditional and infinite. Through the prophet the Lord reminds us: "My thoughts are not your thoughts, / nor are your ways my ways" (Is 55:8).

As shepherds of your flock, you represent all the shepherds in the church today. These are the bishops, priests, parents, teachers, and everyone else who in any way has the care of the flock of Jesus.

You were men of great faith. Your firm faith inspired and motivated you to "go in haste" to Bethlehem. Your unquestioning faith is an inspiration to all of us, encouraging us to respond wholeheartedly to God's call at any time and in any way. Thank you for that compelling example.

You must have been thrilled and overjoyed when the full import of these events dawned upon you. You, like all of Israel, were waiting for the coming of the Messiah. Little did you think that you would be so personally involved in his coming into the world.

TWENTY-SEVEN
To the Angel of the Lord

"'You have nothing to fear! I come to proclaim good news to you, tidings of great joy to be shared by the whole people.'" (Lk 2:10)

I appreciate the message which you brought us from on high. It is a source of great hope and consolation to me and to everyone who knows the message: "I come to proclaim good news to you—tidings of great joy to be shared by the whole people. This day in David's city a savior has been born to you, the Messiah and Lord" (Lk 2:10-11).

There is much to be heard in your message of good news. The good news that all of us want to hear is that we are loved and lovable. "God is love," and we are created in his image and likeness. He shared with us the desire to be loved. It is a natural desire of every human heart. Your message proclaims the most gratifying news anyone could ever hear—that God loves us so much that he gave us the greatest gift he could give in his Son, Jesus. John says it so beautifully: "Yes, God so loved the world [and me] / that he gave us his only Son" (Jn 3:16). Thank you for bringing us such good news.

For ages the shepherds and all the chosen people had waited for the coming of the Redeemer. The long, long Advent had come to an end. God was faithful to all his promises.

Your message was short but full of meaning. You called Mary's first-born the Savior. At that time, names were not chosen at random. The name of a person was very important because it signified the personality or the mission of that individual.

You, or one of your angel hosts, had already prepared Joseph for the naming ceremony. When you came in a dream to assure Joseph that Mary's pregnancy was due to the overshadowing of the Holy Spirit, you also instructed him "to name him Jesus because he will save his people from their sins" (Mt 1:21).

In years to come, even the heretical Samaritans would recognize him as Savior. "We know that this really is the Savior of the world" (Jn 4:42).

You also declared that Jesus is the Savior, "the Messiah and Lord." This title means that he is the "Anointed of the Lord." We use the Greek word *Christus* or a combination of both names—Jesus Christ, Savior and Anointed. After Paul's conversion on the Damascus roadway, he recognized Jesus as Savior, Messiah, and Lord. In his pastoral zeal, he instructs us: "... at Jesus' name / every knee must bend / in the heavens, on the earth, / and under the earth, / and every tongue proclaim / to the glory of God the Father: / JESUS CHRIST IS LORD!" (Phil 2:10f).

TWENTY-EIGHT
Glory to God

"'Glory to God in high heaven.'" (Lk 2:14)

Angels of the highest heaven, you were a specially chosen choir to announce the birth of "the Son of the Most High." In those days it was customary that when a child was born, musicians would gather to welcome him and serenade him. Jesus was probably born in the privacy of a cave away from the crowds assembled for the census-taking. The usual group of serenaders was not at all aware of his coming into the world. It was far more fitting that the birth of Jesus should be hailed by "a multitude of heavenly host, praising God and saying:

> 'Glory to God in high heaven,
> peace on earth to those on whom his favor rests.'"

Your message was much more than a mere announcement of the birth of Jesus. It was in reality a moving proclamation with two distinct messages. In the first statement you were inviting us to give glory to God in high heaven.

As creatures we give glory to God by honoring and praising him. We give glory to God when we acknowledge his power and might. God is glorified when we recognize his divine majesty and splendor. As we thank him for his loving mercy and compassion for us in spite of our sin, we are expressing our "Glory to God in high heaven."

Heavenly Host, you announced Jesus as the Savior of the world. As we confidently trust in his saving power, we are manifesting his glory in our own lives and in the lives of all who will accept him as Savior and Redeemer. You wanted us to know that Jesus would give glory to the Father by his whole lifestyle. You were prophesying that Jesus' supreme and perfect act of glory would be his redemptive death and resurrection. In these words you encouraged us to join you in praising and glorifying our heavenly Father for the gift of Jesus to us.

As Jesus was preparing to enter into his glory, he confirmed this truth at the Last Supper the night before he died. He said to the Father: "I have given you glory on earth / by finishing the work you gave me to do" (Jn 17:4). In the same final discourse to us, Jesus told us that when we strive to fulfill the duties of our state in life, we, too, would be giving glory to God. He told us in these words: "My Father has been glorified / in your bearing much fruit / and becoming my disciples" (Jn 15:8).

All of you, heavenly hosts, were glorifying God by carrying out the will of the Father in bringing us this message—"tidings of great joy to be shared by the whole people" (Lk 2:10).

TWENTY-NINE

The Heavenly Host Announces Peace

"Peace on earth to those on whom his favor rests." (Lk 2:14)

Your choral announcement to the shepherds was intended for all of us. "Peace on earth to those on whom his favor rests," is a profound statement. This is the second phase of your proclamation with its twofold message. It calls to mind the words of the prophet and the various titles attributed to Jesus. "For a child is born to us, a son is given us; / upon his shoulder dominion rests. / They name him Wonder-Counselor, God-Hero, / Father-Forever, Prince of Peace" (Is 9:5).

In your angelic hymn of praise, you were assuring us that the newborn king of the Jews would bring peace into our restless, ruthless world. By his death and resurrection, Jesus gained that peace which the world cannot give.

St. Paul confirms this very clearly: "Now that we have been justified by faith, we are at peace with God through our Lord Jesus Christ" (Rom 5:1). This is the peace you foretold in your message from heaven.

Jesus restored our fragmented relationship with God, a relationship which had been severed when sin entered into the world. This restoration is the source of our peace. When we are at peace with God, then we will be at peace with ourselves, with one another, and with the whole of God's creation.

In your message you informed us that peace would come to those "on whom his favor rests." This is a reminder to us that peace is a gift. God does not reward us because of our own goodness. On the contrary, God bestows goodness on us by his divine mercy and love. We can resist his grace to lead us into goodness, but we cannot merit his grace by our own efforts alone. We need to be cooperative and open to receive his gift. Then we will experience the peace which this world cannot give.

Jesus came into the world as the Prince of Peace. He promised us that his redemptive work would be the source of our peace. " 'Peace' is my farewell to you, / my peace is my gift to you" (Jn 14:27).

Jesus confers his gift of peace on us when he gives us his Holy Spirit. At baptism we become the temples of the Holy Spirit who is dynamic and operative within us, transforming us by his divine life and power. Peace is one of the fruits which he produces within us. Among the fruits of the Spirit, St. Paul mentions explicitly love, joy, and peace.

God's favor rests on us since we have been called to experience and enjoy his gift of peace. Furthermore, we are called to be peacemakers by bringing peace to others. Jesus singled out this part of our mission in his Sermon on the Mount by pronouncing a special beatitude: "Blest too are the peacemakers; they shall be called sons of God" (Mt 5:9).

Every human heart longs for that peace which the world cannot give. Your message direct from heaven assures us that this peace is attainable and that God is anxious to grant it, provided that we are receptive.

THIRTY

Shepherds, Men of Faith

"Let us go over to Bethlehem and see this event which the Lord has made known to us.'. . . The shepherds returned, glorifying and praising God for all they had heard and seen, in accord with what had been told them." (Lk 2:15, 20)

I rejoice at your good fortune that God chose you to be the first to visit the newborn Messiah and Lord. You were very special to God.

I remember that each morning and evening an unblemished lamb was offered to God in the temple. I recall also that these lambs were selected from the flocks in the vicinity of Bethlehem. Even though you could not join in the temple worship regularly, you made a great contribution to the worship of the Lord.

Furthermore, you were men of great faith. Your response to the angel's message was prompt and came without hesitation. Your words are memorable: "Let us go over to Bethlehem and see this event which the Lord has made known to us." And you "went in haste." It required faith to accept such a strange and unusual message.

Your faith was rewarded because your hearts were open to the inspirations of the Holy Spirit. You came, you saw, and you understood. This required great faith on your part. You found only an impoverished couple and a little child as helpless as any other newborn babe. Yet you "understood." You recognized the signs which the angel gave you: "Let this be a sign to you: in a manger you will find an infant wrapped in swaddling clothes" (Lk 2:12). This was your sign and you believed.

God was pleased with your response to this great privilege. You glorified and praised God for all you had seen and heard. This is the prayer that the Lord wants of us—our praise and thanksgiving.

Praise is an ideal way for us to worship God. When we contemplate God's goodness, his holiness, his providential love, our hearts want to sing out his praises. That is what you shepherds did. You were so overcome by the faithfulness and love of the Lord that you "returned glorifying and praising God." In this you were joined by your contemporaries: God was praised by Mary; you heard the heavenly host raising their voices in praising God; likewise, as soon as

Zechariah's speech had returned, he had praised God in that wonderful hymn which has been sung down through the ages.

In the Gospels we discover how pleased Jesus was when he found faith in the people to whom he was ministering. He responded immediately to their needs. To the sinful woman, Jesus said: "Your faith has been your salvation" (Lk 7:50). Jesus was moved by the faith of the community when they brought the paralyzed man to him. "Seeing their faith, Jesus said, 'My friend, your sins are forgiven you'" (Lk 5:20). Jesus was pleased with the faith of blind Bartimaeus and assured him: "Your faith has healed you" (Mk 10:52).

On the other hand, Jesus was deeply disappointed at the lack of faith he saw in so many. When Jesus was expelled from his home town of Nazareth, Matthew tells us: "He did not work many miracles there because of their lack of faith" (Mt 13:58). Or again: "He could work no miracle there ... so much did their lack of faith distress him" (Mk 6:5f).

THIRTY-ONE

Mary Treasured These Things in Her Heart

"Mary treasured all these things and reflected on them in her heart" (Lk 2:19).

Your lifestyle, Mary, is a perfect model of a way of life which challenges us to walk more closely with you on our way to Jesus. I remember the motto: "To Jesus through Mary." You are our exemplar in many different areas of our lives. You are a woman of deep personal prayer. You are truly a contemplative. In fact, you are the model for all Christian prayer.

As all of these events occurred in rapid succession, the people who witnessed them were startled and amazed. On the other hand, you, Mary, experienced these happenings with awe and reverence. I am sure you were taken by surprise when the angel Gabriel asked you to become the mother of the Messiah; when you heard of Zechariah's visit from a heavenly messenger; and when you learned of Elizabeth's fertility and heard her acknowledge you as "the mother of my Lord" (Lk 1:43). You were amazed when the shepherds who saw your Son "understood" even though your newborn Babe was helpless and vulnerable. A sense of wonder permeated the whole countryside.

Mary, your sinlessness enabled the Holy Spirit to prepare your delicate heart and soul for these extraordinary events taking place all around you. Your response was perfectly natural for one who lived so closely united with God. You treasured all these things and reflected on them in your heart.

In your prayer you looked beyond these external happenings. They were for you a window through which you beheld divinity at work. In your prayer of the heart, you recognized the power and presence of the Lord. In your oneness with the Lord, you experienced his magnanimous love being poured out upon all mankind. Your spirit of prayerfulness gave you a deeper, richer understanding of God's mysterious designs unfolding in your midst.

Mary, by your example, you teach us that only in

silence and solitude will we be able to recognize the mystery in all the mundane events about us. Only when we listen with our whole being, as you did, will we come to know the Lord as our loving, caring, and concerned God. Only in quiet, prayerful solitude in the presence of the Lord will we begin to comprehend and discern his will and plan in our lives.

In our age we have made such vast strides in technology that we have lost our sense of wonder. There seems to be little room for the sacred in our secular culture. Many think we do not need God in our self-sufficient society. We are all the poorer for it. It is becoming more difficult for us to be aware of the wonders of his love surrounding us. In order to rediscover the wonders of God, we need to spend some time with him. God is calling all of us into a deeper relationship with him through prayer. There is a longing in every human heart for an experience of God in our lives even though many do not recognize that this yearning is for God. Each day we must be willing to give him some quiet time with a listening heart.

Circumcision of Jesus

"When the eighth day arrived for his circumcision, the name Jesus was given the child, the name the angel had given him before he was conceived." (Lk 2:21)

THIRTY-TWO

They Name Him Jesus

"The name Jesus was given the child." (Lk 2:21)

Mary and Joseph, you were both very solicitous and meticulous about observing every detail of the Law. On the eighth day you had your Son circumcised as the Law prescribed. Jesus was totally exempt from the Law. In fact, he himself was the lawgiver, yet you fulfilled the Law as the Spirit directed you.

Circumcision was an important ceremony. It was considered so important that if the eighth day fell on the Sabbath the ceremony was still to be performed even though every other kind of activity was forbidden.

Joseph, I have often wondered about your feelings since the rite of circumcision formally marked a male child as a member of God's chosen people. It was also a common belief that salvation would come through God's chosen people. In your case, how significant was this ceremony since all the hopes of salvation are made concrete in Jesus, as the angel informed you: "He will save his people from their sins" (Mt 1:21).

The naming ceremony was also important. According to the custom and tradition of your people, the father was to take the child in his arms and give the child his name. This was a meaningful ceremony for both father and son.

Joseph, since you were the father of record, you performed this ceremony and followed the angel's directive in naming him Jesus. You were affirming by this action that you would provide for and protect the Child Jesus; that you would love and educate him.

The Lord does the same for us, as he told us through his prophet: "Fear not, for I have redeemed you; / I have called you by name: you are mine" (Is 43:1).

The name was also important because it symbolized the character or nature of the person. His name would also identify his way of life or the vocation to which the person was called.

How perfectly true this is of Jesus! The original form of the name Jesus is *Yeshua,* which means "Yahweh has saved." It also means "Yeshua brings salvation from God." All this is summed up in the Person of Jesus.

Guests from the East

After Jesus' birth in Bethlehem of Judea during the reign of King Herod, astrologers from the east arrived one day in Jerusalem inquiring, "Where is the newborn king of the Jews? We observed his star at its rising and have come to pay him homage." At this news King Herod became greatly disturbed, and with him all Jerusalem. Summoning all of the chief priests and scribes of the people, he inquired of them where the Messiah was to be born. "In Bethelehem of Judea," they informed him. "Here is what the prophet has written:

'And you, Bethlehem, land of Judah,
*   are by no means least among the princes of Judah,*
*   since from you shall come a ruler*
*   who is to shepherd my people Israel.' "*

Herod called the astrologers aside and found out from them the exact time of the star's appearance. Then he sent them to Bethlehem, after having instructed them: "Go and get detailed information about the child. When you have found him, report it to me so that I may go and offer him homage too."

After their audience with the king, they set out. The star which they had observed at its rising went ahead of them until it came to a standstill over the place where the child was. They were overjoyed at seeing the star, and on entering the house, found the child with Mary his mother. They prostrated themselves and did him homage. Then they opened their coffers and presented him with gifts of gold, frankincense, and myrrh.

They received a message in a dream not to return to Herod, so they went back to their own country by another route. (Mt 2:1-12)

THIRTY-THREE

We Have Seen His Star

"Where is the newborn king of the Jews? We observed his star at its rising and have come to pay him homage.'" (Mt 2:2)

I do not know how to address you, since you are called kings, wisemen, and astrologers. Since you came to seek out Jesus, you are our special friends. You came to worship the newborn king of the Jews, the promised Messiah and Lord.

We are told that you were part of a tribe of priests very similar to the Levites in Israel. You were teachers and instructors. In Persia, a priest had to be present at every sacrifice which was offered. You were highly respected as wise and holy men.

I stand in admiration of your great faith and your perseverance. You left home and traveled a great distance, yet you had very little evidence. You might have had some knowledge of prophecies proclaimed by the Jewish prophets. Were you aware of the prophecy: "A star shall advance from Jacob?" You might have connected the Messiah's birth with the star. As astrologers and astronomers, you spent much time in studying the heavens.

It would be interesting to know how his star differed from the many millions of other stars. Today, some scholars think that it might have been the conjunction of the planets Jupiter and Saturn. Be that as it may, it had to be a spectacular phenomenon to convince you that a king had been born, and you set out to find him.

You had deep, convincing faith. Furthermore, you were humble enough to be receptive to the divine inspiration you received. Your faith was truly a faith of commitment. You believed so strongly that you were willing to undertake all the difficulties of the strenuous travel of those days. You persevered in spite of the hardships of the journey. You wanted to pay homage to the newborn king of the Jews.

Did it surprise you that King Herod pretended to know nothing about the newborn king of the Jews? Were you concerned that he did not go with you in search of the Babe of Bethlehem? Did Herod arouse any suspicions in you about his attitude and his motives? Your great faith is in such contrast to Herod's cynical cunning.

THIRTY-FOUR

Gold, Frankincense, and Myrrh

"They prostrated themselves and did him homage. Then they opened their coffers and presented him with gifts of gold, frankincense, and myrrh." (Mt 2:11)

I am thrilled that you did not let Herod dissuade you.

After you left Herod's palace, you too were over-joyed when the star reappeared, but how much greater was your joy when you found the newborn king of the Jews. I am delighted that you did not get discouraged but persevered in your quest until you "found the child with Mary his Mother."

You followed the custom of your day by bringing him gifts. These were not only precious gifts, but they were highly significant and symbolic. Your choice of gold was ideal, because you recognized him as the king of the Jews. Gold is the gift acknowledging kingship.

When you decided on the gift of frankincense, you must have had some special inspiration. How else could you know that he would be a great priest? You yourselves were priests, and you had great respect for the office of priesthood. Jesus was not only a priest, but he also was destined to become the eternal High Priest, who continues to offer our gifts to the Father at every eucharistic celebration.

The Spirit must have revealed to you that eventually this newborn king would sacrifice his life for the salvation of mankind. Your gift of myrrh manifested your recognition of this child as the Redeemer of the world. Toward the end of your visit, you received a special message from on high warning you not to return to Herod. You did not doubt the authenticity of the message and went back to your own country by another route.

Presentation in the Temple

When the day came to purify them according to the law of Moses, the couple brought him up to Jerusalem so that he could be presented to the Lord, for it is written in the law of the Lord, "Every first-born male shall be consecrated to the Lord." They came to offer in sacrifice "a pair of turtledoves or two young pigeons," in accord with the dictate in the law of the Lord. (Lk 2:22-24)

THIRTY-FIVE

Offering God to God

"The couple brought him up to Jerusalem so that he could be presented to the Lord." (Lk 2:22)

Mary, as you journeyed to the temple to fulfill the requirements of the Law, you radiated the immense joy which filled your heart. You were so proud of your baby. Joseph, everyone must have noticed how fondly and how solicitously you looked on Mary and her treasure from heaven.

Mary, you certainly could have been excused from the law of purification, yet you wanted to fulfill every detail of the Law. The same is true of the law of redemption. Even though your Son was exempt from the law, which required the first-born to be offered to the Lord and then redeemed back by presenting a gift, neither one of you wanted to claim any exemption.

If every child is a gift from God, how infinitely great is the gift of God himself in the Person of Jesus. This was your secret.

Furthermore, although your Son is the Creator, Energizer, and Sustainer of the universe, you could not offer the redemption gift of a lamb. You gladly accepted your poverty. You were not the least bit ashamed to offer " 'a pair of turtle doves or two young pigeons,' in accord with the dictate in the law of the Lord."

The rationale of this law, which stated that the first-born "belonged" to the Lord, was based in the fact that the first-born of your people had been spared in the tenth plague in Egypt, while the Egyptian first-born males were destroyed by the angel at the Passover. Your own first-born was to redeem the world, to deliver all people not from the slavery of Egypt but from the slavery of sin.

Simeon: a Prophet in Waiting

There lived in Jerusalem at the time a certain man named Simeon. He was just and pious, and awaited the consolation of Israel, and the Holy Spirit was upon him. It was revealed to him by the Holy Spirit that he would not experience death until he had seen the Anointed of the Lord. He came to the temple now, inspired by the Spirit; and when the parents brought in the child Jesus to perform for him the customary ritual of the law, he took him in his arms and blessed God in these words:

"Now, Master, you can dismiss your servant in peace;
* you have fulfilled your word.*
For my eyes have witnessed your saving deed
* displayed for all the peoples to see:*
A revealing light to the Gentiles,
* the glory of your people Israel."*

The child's father and mother were marveling at what was being said about him. Simeon blessed them and said to Mary his mother: "This child is destined to be the downfall and the rise of many in Israel, a sign that will be opposed—and you yourself shall be pierced with a sword—so that the thoughts of many hearts may be laid bare." (Lk 2:25-35)

THIRTY-SIX

A Just and Pious Man

"He was just and pious, and awaited the consolation of Israel, and the Holy Spirit was upon him." (Lk 2:25)

How blest we are to know you, Simeon, and the special mission to which the Lord called you and to which you responded so generously.

You were "just and pious." Sacred Scripture does not use such words idly and without a definite purpose. They tell us how much your whole life was in tune with the will of the Lord.

You were always receptive to the working of the Holy Spirit within you. Through his divine influence, you knew the prophecies. Like many of the good Israelites, you prayed fervently and waited patiently for the coming of the promised Messiah.

However, many of your own people believed that since they were the chosen people, they would eventually conquer the world. They had a mistaken idea of the Messiah. They expected a great champion from heaven who would conquer the world by super-natural means.

In contrast to those who dreamed of violence and power, you were one of those quiet people who waited in quiet watchfulness. All your life you prayed and worshiped in the temple in humble and faithful expectation, waiting for the day that the Lord would comfort his people.

What great joy was yours when the Holy Spirit revealed to you that you would not experience death until you had seen the Anointed of the Lord.

As you counted the days and as the months grew into years, you never lost hope. What a lesson for me! When the Lord does not seem to respond immediately to my prayer, I often get discouraged and wonder about the value of my prayer. Thank you for persevering and thus encouraging me never to fear or doubt, never to give up hope.

How tenderly and fondly you took the Child in your arms! Your eyes, no doubt, were misty and your voice trembled as you poured out the prayerful sentiments of your heart.

Simeon, I must remember that Jesus is in my midst always. He is living with me and within me. Jesus came into the world not merely as a guest for a brief stay to redeem us but to stay. He loved us so much, he did not want to leave us. He rose from the dead that he might share his risen glorified life with us. His final word of encouragement to us at the end of Matthew's Gospel assures us of his presence: "Know that I am with you always, until the end of the world!" (Mt 28:20).

At the Last Supper, Jesus offers us comfort and consolation before laying down his life: "I will not leave you orphaned: / I will come back to you" (Jn 14:18). On several occasions St. Paul tells us in no uncertain terms that we are the temples of the Holy Spirit and that the Lord is dwelling with us and within us.

THIRTY-SEVEN

Simeon's Hymn of Joyful Acceptance

" 'Now, Master, you can dismiss your servant in peace; / you have fulfilled your word. / For my eyes have witnessed your saving deed.' " (Lk 2:29-30)

How much I appreciate your powerful prayer which begins with the words: "Now, Master, you can dismiss your servant in peace. . . ." This manifests the beauty of your soul and proves that you are a "just and pious" person.

I am deeply moved by your gracious spirit of resignation and willingness to accept the Lord's will when he called you to himself. Since your will was in such harmony with his divine will, you were at peace with God, with yourself, and with the world around you. In this prayer you were asking for an everlasting peace.

Your joy ran over in a genuine spirit of gratefulness. You had been waiting patiently throughout your whole lifetime for the fulfillment of the Lord's promise to send a Savior and Redeemer. Now you perceived that the Lord was fulfilling his word.

All your life you were so open and receptive to the Holy Spirit that you immediately recognized the humble Babe of Bethlehem as the fulfillment of all the messianic prophecies, promises, and prayers. Guided by the Holy Spirit, you were also aware that he was to be "a revealing light to the Gentiles." This was really a prophetic utterance. You understood that all people are called to salvation.

Simeon, you clearly understood that Jesus was to bring salvation to the whole world. That salvation would cost him his life. Speaking of his crucifixion, Jesus prophesied: "I—once I am lifted up from earth— / will draw all men to myself" (Jn 12:32). As the Good Shepherd, he also told us that he was freely laying down his life for us and that his redeeming love would bring us eternal life. "I came that they might have life / and have it to the full" (Jn 10:10). Finally, a few hours before he died he prayed for our salvation: "Father, / all those you gave me / I would have in my company / where I am, / to see this glory of mine" (Jn 17:24).

THIRTY-EIGHT

The Shadow of the Cross

"This child is destined to be the downfall and the rise of many in Israel, a sign that will be opposed." (Lk 2:34)

Simeon, what mixed emotions filled your heart when you blessed Mary and Joseph. You tried to prepare them for the things that would eventually happen. You were inspired by the Holy Spirit in this prophecy.

You knew that the Messiah would be "a sign that will be opposed." You were also aware that many of your own people would reject him because their notion of the Messiah was different. Many would not only reject him but would be very hostile to him.

On the other hand, as you said, he would be "the rise of many in Israel." Many would believe in him, follow his way of life, and reach their eternal happiness. Yes, there would be a great rejection, but there would also be a marvelous acceptance.

Your prophecy gave us a foreshadowing of the universal salvation which Jesus came to proclaim. You also prepared us for the necessity of suffering in our lives as we join in Jesus' redemptive mission. I am sure that Mary and Joseph saw the shadow of the cross over their little family.

Did you hesitate to tell Mary that she would be asked to endure suffering as sharp as a piercing sword? These are hard and strange words, but you wanted Mary to realize that she, too, had a painful role to play in the redemption of the world.

In the devotional life of the church, we commemorate Mary's sevenfold sorrows on the Feast of Our Lady of Sorrows, celebrated on September 15.

The first of these sorrows, Simeon, is your own prophecy of the sword which would pierce her heart. Her second sorrow is the exile in Egypt to escape Herod when he tried to dispose of the Child Jesus. The loss of Jesus in the temple at the age of twelve is the third sorrow. The last four concern the passion and death of Jesus: Jesus meeting his Mother at the fourth station, the crucifixion, the taking down of his body from the cross, and finally the pain of separation experienced in his burial.

Anna the Prophetess

There was also a certain prophetess, Anna by name, daughter of Phanuel of the tribe of Asher. She had seen many days, having lived seven years with her husband after her marriage and then as a widow until she was eighty-four. She was constantly in the temple worshiping day and night in fasting and prayer. Coming on the scene at this moment, she gave thanks to God and talked about the child to all who looked forward to the deliverance of Jerusalem. (Lk 2:36-38)

THIRTY-NINE

A Lifetime of Prayer

"She [Anna] was constantly in the temple, worshiping day and night in fasting and prayer." (Lk 2:37)

Anna, you enjoyed only seven short years of married life and spent long years as a widow. According to the common belief of your day, to lose a spouse and thus terminate a family was regarded as a sign of God's disfavor.

During your years of widowhood, you thus experienced sorrow and loneliness. You must have been persecuted by your self-righteous neighbors and friends, yet you did not grow bitter. Sorrow can make us hard, calloused, bitter, resentful, even rebellious against God. This did not happen to you.

On the contrary, sorrow made you kinder, gentler, holier, more prayerful, and more lovingly concerned about others. Sorrow sometimes robs people of their faith. But in your case, sorrow enriched and deepened your faith. This happened because of your personal relationship with the Lord.

You thought of God as a gracious, loving Father who "knows well the plans" he has in mind for you, "plans for your welfare, not for woe" (Jer 29:11f). This awareness of God's great love for you transformed you into a gracious, loving person. I admire, love, and respect you for your openness to what the Lord wanted to accomplish in you.

Anna, you were eighty years of age, but you were young at heart. You were blessed with a vibrant hope. You never thought of God as distant or detached. Your hope never faded.

What made you such a remarkable person? What kept you so young at heart, so enthusiastic, so full of hope? The answer lies in the Scriptures. You were "constantly in the temple, worshiping day and night in fasting and prayer."

The years did not change your disposition. You were not bitter, nor was your hope ever daunted, because each day you met the Lord in prayer. Yours was a faith of expectancy. Your rich personal relationship with your loving Father removed all doubt and fear of disappointment.

Anna, you fasted daily, which contributed much to the intensity of your prayer. Fasting is an ideal prayer posture because it keeps us more aware of the presence of the Lord and his loving care and concern for us.

You not only spent long hours in prayer alone with the Lord, but you also participated in the temple worship. You prayed together with your own people. Someone has said: "They pray best together who first pray alone." That is precisely the method you followed.

FORTY

Anna Proclaims the Good News

"Coming on the scene at this moment, she [Anna] gave thanks to God and talked about the child to all who looked forward to the deliverance of Jerusalem." (Lk 2:38)

What a tremendous thrill it must have been for you when Mary and Joseph arrived with the Child Jesus. It must have been the Holy Spirit who inspired you to come "on the scene" at that moment.

The joy which surged through your whole being must have been great. Your dreams, hopes, and expectations of all the long years were fulfilled in this great moment of salvation history. Deep within your being, you must have been jubilant and ecstatic. The dream of your lifetime was unfolding before you.

Your response was exactly what we would expect from such a saintly person. You thanked God and spread the Good News of salvation "to all who looked forward to the deliverance of Jerusalem."

From your place in heaven, you must know that your example and influence have come down to us throughout the centuries. Today there is a host of wonderful "Annas" who are following your way of life. They draw their inspiration and encouragement from you. Every parish, every community, every extended family, has its "Annas." They continually present their list of petitions to the Lord on behalf of the needs of so many of us.

Their love and devotion, their prayers and sacrifices, bring untold blessings upon all of us. Like you, they continually thank God for the outpouring of his manifold blessings upon us. They never hesitate to spread the Good News of God's love to anyone and everyone who will listen.

Like you, Anna, they are the hope of the church. Like you, they are kind, gracious, and sympathetic because they follow your example of constant prayer sent heavenward.

Their simple but deep faith is a challenging example for all of us. They live with the faith of expectancy, knowing at the core of their being that God's love will permeate all the affairs of life.

Other Books of Interest from Servant Publications

Basics of the Faith
A Catholic Catechism
by Alan Schreck

A concise and reliable catechism for today's reader, with a foreword by John Cardinal O'Connor. An up-to-date and readable guide to the teaching of the church. *$8.95*

Scriptural Prayer Journal
Learning to Meditate on the Bible Each Day
by David E. Rosage

An excellent one-year guide. Teaching on how to meditate on the Bible, a Scripture passage for each day, and a journal to enable the reader to record personal reflections for each passage. *$6.95*

Draw Near to God
Daily Meditations by Pope John Paul II

Encouragement, instruction, and inspiration from Pope John Paul II for each day of the year. *$7.95*